This book belongs to:

....

 I read this book once!

 I read this book twice!

 I read this book three times!

Retold by Gaby Goldsack
Illustrated by Ruth Galloway

Language consultants: Betty Root and Monica Hughes

This edition published by Parragon in 2007
Parragon
Queen Street House
4 Queen Street
Bath BA1 1HE, UK

ISBN 978-1-4054-9324-6

Printed in China

The Ugly Duckling

Bath New York Singapore Hong Kong Cologne Delhi Melbourne

Notes for Parents

These **Gold Stars**® reading books encourage and support children who are learning to read.

Starting to read

• Start by reading the book aloud to your child. Take time to talk about the pictures. They often give clues about the story. The easy-to-read speech bubbles provide an excellent 'joining-in' activity.

• Over time, try to read the same book several times. Gradually your child will want to read the book aloud with you. It helps to run your finger under the words as you say them.

• Occasionally, stop and encourage your child to continue reading aloud without you. Join in again when your child needs help. This is the next step towards helping your child become an independent reader.

• Finally, your child will be ready to read alone. Listen carefully and give plenty of praise. Remember to make reading an enjoyable experience.

Using your stickers
Remember to use the **Gold Stars**® stickers at the front of the book as a reward for effort as well as achievement.

The fun colour stickers in the centre of the book and fold-out scene board at the back will help your child re-enact parts of the story, again and again.

Remember these four stages:
• Read the story **to** your child.

• Read the story **with** your child.

• Encourage your child to read **to you**.

• Listen to your child read **alone**.

7

crack!

8

One day a mother duck sat on her nest.

She was waiting for her eggs to hatch.

She waited and waited.

Then, crack! They started to hatch.

Out popped three fluffy yellow ducklings.

Now there was just one egg left.

It was a very big egg.

The mother duck sat back down.

Come on, hatch!

She waited and waited.

She thought it would never hatch.

Then, crack! It started to hatch.

Out popped a big grey duckling.

crack!

The grey duckling looked big and ugly.

The mother duck took her new ducklings
down to the pond.

She showed them how to swim.

Soon they could all swim.

Even the big grey duckling.

The mother duck was very pleased.

The mother duck took her new
ducklings up to the farm.
All the animals thought the grey
duckling was ugly.

You are
ugly!

"What an ugly duckling!" they said.

So the ugly duckling ran away.

He ran to the other side of the pond.

Wild ducks lived on the other side
of the pond.

The wild ducks thought the grey
duckling was ugly.

"What an ugly duckling!" they said.

So the ugly duckling ran away.

He ran to a cottage.

An old woman lived in the cottage.

She lived with a cat and a hen.

The cat and the hen thought the big duckling was ugly.

"What an ugly duckling!" they said.

So the ugly duckling ran away.

He ran to the lake.

One day he saw some

swans fly by.

They were beautiful.

"I wish I looked like that,"

said the ugly duckling.

They are beautiful.

21

Winter came. It grew colder and colder.

The lake turned to ice.

The ugly duckling got stuck in the ice.

A farmer found him.

He took him home.

The farmer's children wanted to play with
the ugly duckling.

The ugly duckling was frightened.

So the duckling ran away.

He ran back to the pond.

He stayed there until spring.

The sun came out. The ugly duckling flapped his wings. They felt strong.

He flapped and flapped until he was
flying high in the air.

The ugly duckling flew back to the lake.

He saw three beautiful swans on the lake.

The ugly duckling landed on the lake.

He looked at himself in the lake.

He was not an ugly duckling.

He was a beautiful swan.

"Be our friend!" said the other swans.

The ugly duckling had some friends at last.

Read and Say

How many of these words can you say?
The pictures will help you. Look back
in your book and see if you can
find the words in the story.

cottage

swans

cat

eggs

pond

farm

duck

ducklings

hen

farmer